Great British

Women

raintree
a Capstone company — publishers for children

Author note

The Great Britons listed in this book have been ordered by their date of birth. Many of the women included were born in the 20th century. For most of the last 2,000 years, women were thought to be weak and incapable of intellectual thoughts and ideas. In the 19th century, some men even suggested that too much education might mean a woman wouldn't be able to have children! Therefore, it's probably not surprising that opportunities for women to be creative outside the home were few and far between.

Diversity

The people included in this book come from a wide range of backgrounds and jobs, but you may have noticed that most of them are white! As with the difficulties faced by women, ethnic minorities have had to deal with prejudice and the resulting lack of opportunities. Gradually, though, people are paying less attention to the colour of a person's skin, or to their gender. Hopefully, if a book was created like this one in, say, 50 years' time, it would be more representative of the true make-up of Britain.

Who have we missed out?

Are there important people you think we've missed out? If so, let us know! The idea was to cover lots of different professions and areas of life as well as including a mix of ethnicities. For the men, in particular, there were many who had to be left out for space reasons, but who deserved to be included. How about King Henry VIII, for example? Or Joseph Lister? David Beckham, perhaps?

Hopefully, the mini biographies in this book will inspire you to find out more about these amazing people. And you could also try to learn about those you think should have been included.

Boudicca

Born: AD 30, East Anglia
Died: AD 61, unknown

Warrior queen

After her husband died, Boudicca became queen of the Iceni people in the east of England. However, the Romans (who had invaded Britain in AD 43) decided they wanted the Iceni lands. Boudicca led her people and other nearby tribes to fight the Romans. They fought successful battles and destroyed Roman towns. Finally, Roman general Gaius Suetonius Paulinus defeated Boudicca and her warriors.

Queen Elizabeth I

Born: 1533, London
Died: 1603, Richmond

Long-reigning queen

Elizabeth became queen in 1558. She ruled alone, which was unusual for a queen during those times. Elizabeth had to deal with several threats to her reign. These included Catholics, who wanted Mary, Queen of Scots – Elizabeth's cousin – to be queen. Elizabeth had Mary executed in 1587. In 1588, England faced the invading Spanish Armada. After a stirring speech from Elizabeth, her navy defeated the Spanish ships. Elizabeth's reign was a long and successful one.

Mary Wollstonecraft

Born: 1759, London
Died: 1797, London

Author

In 1784, Mary Wollstonecraft set up a school with her sisters and a friend, but it didn't prove successful. She then became a **governess** in Ireland. A friend, Joseph Johnson, gave her money to help her write her first book. It was about educating girls. From 1788, Wollstonecraft worked as a reviewer and editor on Johnson's *Analytical Review* magazine. Wollstonecraft's best-known book, *A Vindication of the Rights of Woman*, was published in 1792. She believed that girls should be educated in a way that would allow them to earn their own living when older. She wanted equality for women. This was the first time that a book had been written about this subject.

FAST FACT

Wollstonecraft was the mother of Mary Shelley, author of *Frankenstein* (1818).

Jane Austen

Born: 1775, Steventon, Hampshire
Died: 1817, Winchester

Author

In 1811, *Sense and Sensibility*, Jane Austen's first novel, was published. A London publisher had rejected *First Impressions*, a story that we now know as *Pride and Prejudice*, in 1797. Her novels were about middle and upper-class life. They were published **anonymously**: only friends and family knew she had written them. This was because writing books wasn't thought to be an acceptable activity for a woman. It is thought that over 20 million copies of *Pride and Prejudice* alone have been sold.

Elizabeth Fry

Born: 1780, Earlham, Norfolk
Died: 1845, Ramsgate, Kent

Campaigner

Elizabeth Fry worked at local charities from the age of 18. In 1812, she visited Newgate Prison for the first time, even spending a night there. She was shocked by how bad conditions were. Fry

encouraged prisoners to look after themselves better. In 1817, Fry set up the Association for the **Reformation** of the Female Prisoners in Newgate. It was one of the first women's organizations in Britain. Fry played an important role in getting a law passed in 1823 that improved prison conditions. Her efforts didn't end with prisons. She also set up a shelter for the homeless in London.

Mary Anning

Born: 1799, Lyme Regis, Dorset
Died: 1847, Lyme Regis, Dorset

Palaeontologist - fossil hunter

Mary Anning lived in an area of Dorset that had many fossils from the Jurassic Period (about 201 to 145 million years ago). Mary's family was very poor. They sold fossils to tourists, collectors and scientists. In 1811–1812, Mary and her brother found a complete Ichthyosaur. Mary's major finds included the first complete skeleton of a Plesiosaurus, discovered in 1823, and a Pterodactylus in 1828. Mary became an expert in many subjects (including dinosaur poo!) but she wasn't given scientific credit for her finds.

Ada Lovelace

Born: 1815, London
Died: 1852, London

Mathematician

As a girl, Lovelace was taught mathematics. This was unusual for the time. In 1833, she met and worked with Charles Babbage. He was working on a Difference Engine, an early computer. She worked closely with him on the project. It is not known how great Lovelace's contribution was. But she translated an article about an Analytical Engine from French to English. She added notes, including steps for solving a mathematical problem. She then became known as "the first computer programmer". Lovelace realized that computers might be used for more than just mathematics.

Brontë sisters

Charlotte born: 1816, Thornton, Yorkshire   Died: 1855, Haworth
Emily born: 1818, Thornton, Yorkshire   Died: 1848, Haworth
Anne born: 1820, Thornton, Yorkshire   Died: 1849, Scarborough

Authors

The Brontë sisters began writing stories from a young age. All the sisters lived away from home at times in order to teach. But by 1845, all the family were living at Haworth, the family home in Yorkshire. They all wrote novels: Charlotte wrote *Jane Eyre* (1847), Emily wrote *Wuthering Heights* (1847) and Anne wrote *The Tenant of Wildfell Hall* (1848). In 1848–1849, their brother, Branwell, died and so did Emily and Anne. Charlotte continued to write novels until her marriage in 1854.

FAST FACT

In 1846, Charlotte, Emily and Anne published a book of poetry, but not under their own names: they used Currer, Ellis and Acton Bell. This was because of an experience Charlotte had had when sending her poetry to the **Poet Laureate**, Robert Southey. He replied: "Literature cannot be the business of a woman's life, and it ought not to be."

Queen Victoria

Born: 1819, London
Died: 1901, East Cowes, Isle of Wight

Long-serving queen

Victoria was just 18 years old when she became queen. She married Prince Albert in 1840. They had nine children, although Victoria didn't enjoy motherhood. Victoria was devastated when Albert died in 1861. After he died she always wore black as a sign of mourning. In 1877, Victoria became Empress of India. This title was to show the link between the British monarchy and its Empire, which included India. Victoria now ruled a quarter of the world. She was on the throne for more than 63 years, longer than any other king or queen to that point.

Florence Nightingale

Born: 1820, Florence, Italy
Died: 1910, London

Nurse, social reformer

Florence Nightingale and her sister were educated by their father. Nightingale was very good at science and maths. After doing nursing training in Germany, she got a job at a women's hospital in London. During the Crimean War (1853–1856), Nightingale took 38 nurses by ship to Scutari, Turkey. She worked to improve the terrible conditions for injured soldiers in army hospitals. After the war, Nightingale investigated army hospital deaths. She discovered that most could have been prevented by keeping hospitals and equipment clean. Nightingale used her maths skills to create the first "rose" diagram to force the government to clean up hospitals. In 1859, Nightingale published two books about nursing. A nursing school was set up the following year. Nightingale helped to make nursing a **profession**.

Isabella Bird

Born: 1831, Boroughbridge, Yorkshire
Died: 1904, Edinburgh

Explorer, travel writer and photographer

In her youth, Isabella Bird suffered from poor health. In her twenties, a doctor suggested she go on a long sea journey, so she travelled to the United States in 1854. Afterwards, Bird wrote a book called *An Englishwoman in America*. She travelled to many countries, including Australia, Hawaii and China. Bird wrote books about her travels and her later books included her own photographs of the places she visited. Bird became the first female member of the Royal Geographical Society in 1892.

FAST FACT

Bird once wrote a letter home that was 116 pages long!

Elizabeth Garrett Anderson

Born: 1836, London
Died: 1917, Aldeburgh, Suffolk

Doctor

Elizabeth Garrett Anderson wanted to be a doctor, but no medical schools would allow her to study because she was a woman. She became a nursing student and went to medical classes for men, but they complained, so she had to stop going. Anderson passed the Society of **Apothecaries** examination in 1865 and became a medical attendant at St Mary's Dispensary in London. She then taught herself French so she could go to France and qualify as a doctor there. The British Medical Register still refused to accept her. In 1872, she set up the New Hospital for Women at St Mary's Dispensary. Anderson campaigned for women to become doctors. In 1876, this finally became possible.

Octavia Hill

Born: 1838, Wisbech, Cambridgeshire
Died: 1912, London

Housing reformer, co-founder of National Trust

Octavia Hill's family was interested in helping others. In 1864, the art critic John Ruskin bought three run-down houses in London. He gave them to Octavia Hill to manage. Once repaired, those houses were rented to poor people. Hill managed hundreds of houses around London. She also taught other women how to manage housing projects. Hill was also involved in the open spaces movement. The poorer areas of London were overcrowded, so she wanted to make sure that open spaces were available for everyone. Hill **co-founded** the National Trust for Places of Historic Interest or Natural Beauty in 1895.

Gertrude Jekyll

Born: 1843, London
Died: 1932, Munstead Heath, Surrey

Garden designer, author

Gertrude Jekyll was a talented painter and went to art school in London. When her mother built a house in Munstead Heath in 1876, Jekyll designed the gardens. Garden experts were soon visiting to see her work. She used her knowledge of plants and her artist's view of colour to make gardens appear natural. She also selected and bred plants. Jekyll met **architect** Sir Edwin Lutyens in 1889 and they worked together on many projects. From 1881, Jekyll wrote over 1,000 articles for magazines such as *Country Life*. She also wrote books. Jekyll designed over 400 gardens in Britain, Europe and the United States.

E. Nesbit

Born: 1848, London
Died: 1924, Dymchurch, Kent

Author

In 1880, Edith Nesbit married Hubert Bland, a man who had strong political beliefs. Nesbit herself was a **socialist**. They co-founded the Fabian Society in 1884. Nesbit wrote about socialism and gave talks on the subject during the 1880s. Nesbit had begun writing while a teenager and had had a poem published. In the early years of her marriage, it was the success of her children's stories that allowed the family to move to a bigger house. Nesbit wrote more than 60 children's books, including *Five Children and It* (1902) and *The Railway Children* (1906).

Emmeline Pankhurst

Born: 1858, Manchester
Died: 1928, London

Suffragette

Emmeline Pankhurst married Richard Pankhurst, a supporter of the women's suffrage movement. This movement called for women to be allowed to vote in elections. Pankhurst set up the Women's Franchise League in 1889. She then helped to found the Women's Social and Political Union (WSPU) in 1903. Christabel and Sylvia, Emmeline's daughters, were also involved. Members of this organization were called suffragettes. They became known for carrying out violent demonstrations. Once arrested – as Pankhurst was a number of times – they would refuse to eat. This led to the women being fed by force. Finally, in 1918, women over the age of 30 were allowed to vote. However, it was 1928 before women were given equal voting rights with men.

Mary Kingsley

Born: 1862, London
Died: 1900, Simonstown, South Africa

Explorer, author

At the age of 30, Mary Kingsley travelled to Africa. She made her way into land that no European, let alone a woman, had ever been. She used local people as her guides. Kingsley collected beetles and fish for the British Museum and, on her return to Britain, gave talks about her experiences. Kingsley was adventurous and later climbed Mount Cameroon in Cameroon, Africa. She was the first woman to do so. Kingsley died of a fever while nursing during the Boer War (1899–1902).

FAST FACT

As a girl, Kingsley blew up a tub of manure (animal poo). She was trying to make gunpowder but instead just made a mess on a line of clean washing!

Edith Cavell

Born: 1865, Swardeston, Norfolk
Died: 1915, Belgium

Nurse

Edith Cavell worked as a governess in Belgium. Returning to England, she cared for her sick father and he encouraged her to become a nurse. She finished her nursing training in 1907 and returned to Belgium to set up a nursing school. During World War I, Cavell nursed all soldiers, not just the British. Some people criticized her for this. Cavell was arrested for helping soldiers to escape from Belgium. She was found guilty and shot by a German firing squad.

Gertrude Bell

Born: 1868, Durham
Died: 1926, Baghdad, Iraq

Traveller, author, archaeologist

Gertrude Bell travelled through the Middle East, writing about her experiences in many books. After World War I, Bell used her knowledge to give the British government advice about dividing the Arab world into new countries. She helped to create the country now known as Iraq. While in the Middle East, Bell always tried to understand the local people and culture. She found many historical items that she gave to a museum in Baghdad rather than sending them to Britain.

FAST FACT

Bell was adventurous and climbed a number of mountains, including Mont Blanc in the Alps.

Emily Wilding Davison

Born: 1872, London
Died: 1913, Epsom, Surrey

Suffragette

After studying at Oxford University, Emily Wilding Davison became a suffragette when she joined the Women's Social and Political Union (WSPU) in 1906. She gave up teaching in order to work solely for the WSPU. She was often arrested for actions such as burning post boxes. While a prisoner at Strangeways Prison, Manchester, she refused to eat. In 1913, Davison ran in front of the king's horse at the Derby, a famous horse race. She later died from her injuries. It is now thought that she wasn't trying to kill herself but to attach a scarf to the king's horse.

Dame Agatha Christie

Born: 1890, Torquay
Died: 1976, Winterbrook, Oxfordshire

Author, playwright

Working as a nurse during World War I, Agatha Christie learnt about the poisons that she later included in her crime novels. She wrote her first book – *The Mysterious Affair at Styles* – in 1920. Although she also wrote romance novels, Christie is best known for her murder mysteries featuring the characters Hercule Poirot and Miss Marple. About 2 billion copies of Christie's books have been sold worldwide.

Amy Johnson

Born: 1903, Hull
Died: 1941, London

Pilot

In 1928, Amy Johnson took flying lessons, a decision that changed her life. She gained her pilot's licence and became the first woman to become a **ground engineer**. In

1930, Johnson became the first woman to fly solo from Britain to Australia. During World War II (1939–1945), she joined the Air Transport Auxiliary, flying machinery and people wherever they needed to go. In 1941, bad weather forced Johnson's plane into the Thames Estuary, where she drowned.

Dame Barbara Hepworth

Born: 1903, Wakefield, Yorkshire
Died: 1975, St Ives, Cornwall

Artist, **sculptor**

Barbara Hepworth had early success exhibiting art in joint shows with her first husband and then second husband, who were both artists. She finally got

The Family of Man, *1970*

her first solo show in 1943. She moved to St Ives in 1939 and continued to live there for the rest of her life. Hepworth is best known for her holed sculptures. She is one of the few women sculptors to become internationally successful.

Dorothy Hodgkin

Born: 1910, Cairo, Egypt
Died: 1994, Crab Mill, Warwickshire

Chemist, X-ray crystallographer

In 1945, Hodgkin used X-ray crystallography to discover the **structure** of **penicillin**. In 1954, she discovered vitamin B12's structure. These achievements led to Hodgkin winning the Nobel Prize for Chemistry in 1964. She is the only British woman to have won this science prize. Hodgkin also published the structure of **insulin** in 1969. Hodgkin was given the Order of Merit, the UK's highest honour, in 1965.

Dame Margot Fonteyn

Born: 1919, Reigate, Surrey
Died: 1991, Panama City, Panama

Ballerina

Margot Fonteyn studied ballet from the age of five. Her first professional appearance came in 1934 at what is now the Royal Ballet. The following year, she became their leading ballerina (the prima ballerina). Fonteyn danced many roles such as Aurora in *The Sleeping Beauty*. But she also created roles in new ballets, such as *Ondine*. Later in her career, she was known for her dance partnership with Russian dancer Rudolf Nureyev. They first performed together in *Giselle* in 1962. Fonteyn continued dancing until she was 60. This was because she needed the money from her dancing to care for her husband, who had been shot and paralysed.

Rosalind Franklin

Born: 1920, London
Died: 1958, London

Chemist, X-ray crystallographer

Rosalind Franklin studied Chemistry at Cambridge University. To continue her studies, she researched the structure of carbon and coal. From 1947 to 1950, Franklin worked in Paris, again studying carbon, but this time using X-rays. X-rays show how a substance is made up. Working in London from 1951, Franklin used X-rays to investigate the structure of **DNA**. This work helped two scientists, Crick and Watson, to discover that DNA is shaped like a double helix, or twisted ladder. Franklin died before the other scientists were awarded the Nobel Prize in 1962.

Margaret Thatcher

Born: 1925, Grantham, Lincolnshire
Died: 2013, London

Politician

Margaret Thatcher studied chemistry at Oxford University. She then trained as a lawyer, before becoming a **Member of Parliament (MP)** in 1959. In 1975, she became the first woman to be chosen as Conservative Party leader. Thatcher won three general elections in a row from 1979. She was the first female Prime Minister and was in office for 11 years. This made her the longest-serving Prime Minister of the 20th century. In 1990, Thatcher was forced to resign when her leadership was challenged. She wrote two autobiographies and gave talks around the world.

Queen Elizabeth II

Born: 1926, London

Longest-reigning British monarch

In 1936, King Edward VIII, Elizabeth's uncle, decided he no longer wanted to be king. This had never happened before and was a shock to the nation. Elizabeth's father had to take the throne, as George VI. When her father died in 1952, Elizabeth became queen. At that time, the royal family was very popular. Gradually, through the 1990s, their popularity fell. Some people even called for the royal family to be scrapped. In 1997, many people were angry at the way the queen reacted to the death of Princess Diana. Since then, however, the royal family's popularity has grown. In 2016, Elizabeth became the longest-reigning monarch in British history.

FAST FACT

In 1945, Elizabeth was a driver and mechanic in the Women's Royal Auxiliary Territorial Service. This was during World War II.

Shirley Williams

Born: 1930, London

Politician

Shirley Williams' early career involved working as a newspaper journalist. She tried several times to become a Member of Parliament (MP) for the Labour Party but wasn't successful until 1964. Labour were in power and by 1967, she was minister of education and science. In 1981, Williams co-founded a new political party called the Social Democratic Party (SDP). The SDP later joined with the Liberal Party to become the Liberal Democrats. Williams was made a **baroness** in 1993. She was leader of the Liberal Democrats in the House of Lords from 2001 to 2004, and finally retired in 2016. Williams taught at Harvard, a top American university, from 1988.

Dame Jane Goodall

Born: 1934, London

Primatologist

Jane Goodall worked as a secretary for Louis Leakey, a well-known scientist. It was Leakey who suggested Goodall study chimpanzees. In 1960, she set off to the forest of Gombe in Tanzania. Goodall appeared to a particular group of chimpanzees at the same time in the same place for two years. Eventually, they began to trust her. She copied their way of life, spending time in trees and eating the same food. She was able to learn more about them than anyone had before. For example, she was the first to realize that chimpanzees make and use tools. Goodall now gives talks around the world about the importance of protecting chimpanzees and about other environmental concerns.

Dame Judi Dench

Born: 1934, York

Actress

Judi Dench's early career focused on the theatre. She won the first of eight Laurence Olivier awards in 1977 for playing Lady Macbeth in the Shakespeare play *Macbeth*. As well as appearing in several long-running television series, including *A Fine Romance* with her husband, Michael Williams, she has appeared in many films. She has been nominated for an Oscar seven times and won Best Supporting Actress for the film *Shakespeare in Love* in 1998. From 1995 to 2012, she played M in the James Bond films.

Dame Maggie Smith

Born: 1934, Ilford, Essex

Actress

In 1964, Maggie Smith appeared with Laurence Olivier in the Shakespeare play *Othello* at the National Theatre in London. She went on to perform in many other plays there during the 1960s. Smith won the first of her two Oscars for the film *The Prime of Miss Jean Brodie* in 1969. She has been nominated for Oscars four more times, including Best Supporting Actress for her role in *Gosford Park* in 2001. Her role in television series *Downton Abbey* won her many more awards.

Dame Shirley Bassey

Born: 1937, Cardiff, Wales

Singer

After being spotted singing in a local club by band leader Jack Hylton, Shirley Bassey got a record deal. She had her first top ten hit in 1957 and a first number one with "As I Love You" in 1959. In the 1960s, Bassey became popular in the United States, particularly after the release of her song "Goldfinger" from the James Bond film. In 1997, Bassey gained new fans by recording "History Repeating" with Propellerheads. Bassey is best known for her recording of three James Bond theme songs: "Goldfinger", "Diamonds are Forever" and "Moonraker". She is thought to have sold 135 million records worldwide.

Dame Anita Roddick

Born: 1942, Littlehampton, West Sussex
Died: 2007, Chichester, West Sussex

Businesswoman, environmental campaigner

Anita Roddick ran a restaurant and hotel with her husband for several years. Then, in 1976, she set up The Body Shop, selling make-up and toiletries made with natural ingredients. Roddick believed that the environment and local people were important. She recycled and reused containers. The business grew until there were over 2,000 shops worldwide. In 2006, Roddick sold The Body Shop to the company L'Oréal for £652 million. She continued to work on environmental campaigns.

FAST FACT

In 1990, Roddick helped to set up *The Big Issue*, the magazine sold by homeless people.

Dame Jocelyn Bell Burnell

Born: 1943, Belfast, Northern Ireland

Physicist, astronomer

After gaining a **physics** degree, Jocelyn Bell Burnell continued her education at the University of Cambridge from 1965. She worked as a research assistant under Anthony Hewish and Martin Ryle. Bell Burnell helped to build a huge radio telescope that would follow quasars. Quasars are brightly lit objects in space that produce radio waves. By 1967, the radio telescope was working, and Bell Burnell's job was to analyse the results. She noticed some patterns that didn't match what they were expecting. Bell Burnell had discovered **radio pulsars**. However, while Hewish and Ryle were awarded the Nobel Prize in 1974, Bell Burnell was ignored. She has gone on to win many other awards, however, and has taught at a number of universities.

Diana, Princess of Wales

Born: 1961, Sandringham, Norfolk
Died: 1997, Paris, France

Campaigner

After Lady Diana Spencer left school, she worked as a nursery school assistant in London. Diana began a relationship with Prince Charles, Queen Elizabeth II's eldest son, in 1980. They married in 1981 and had two children, Princes William and Harry. Diana was very popular and this helped to make the royal family more popular too. She worked hard for many charities, including those connected with the disease AIDS. In 1996, Diana and Charles divorced. Diana continued with her charity work, campaigning for **landmines** to be banned. In 1997, Diana was killed after a car chase through Paris. Photographers had been trying to get photos of Diana with her boyfriend.

Malorie Blackman

Born: 1962, London

Author

Malorie Blackman originally worked in computers. Then, in 1990, she brought out her first book – a collection of short stories for children called *Not So Stupid!* Blackman writes children's stories for all ages, including *Noughts & Crosses*, the popular series of books for young adults. She has written children's TV drama and a play. Blackman has won many awards for her work, including the book and television series *Pig-Heart Boy*. From 2013 to 2015, she was **Children's Laureate**.

J.K. Rowling

Born: 1965, Yate, Gloucestershire

Author

Joanne Rowling first came up with the idea of a boy wizard in 1990 while waiting for a train. The first Harry Potter novel, *Harry Potter and the Philosopher's Stone*, was published in 1997. It was successful and won many awards. The following six books in the series also sold well, making Rowling one of the richest women in Britain. The Harry Potter books have been published in 60 languages. In 2001, a film based on the first of the books was made and broke records. It made more than £16 million in Britain in the first weekend alone. Rowling writes novels for adults too.

Baroness Tanni Grey-Thompson

Born: 1969, Cardiff, Wales

Athlete

Carys Davina Grey-Thompson, known as Tanni, was born with a medical condition called spina bifida. It meant she wasn't able to use her legs. She decided by the age of 13 that she wanted to take part in wheelchair racing. Four years later, Grey-Thompson was part of the British Wheelchair Racing Squad. After winning an Olympic bronze medal in 1988, she went on to win 11 Paralympic gold medals. She also broke 30 world records during her career. Now, Grey-Thompson is a politician in the House of Lords and a TV presenter.

FAST FACT

Tanni's name came about because her older sister nicknamed her 'Tiny' when she first saw her. This nickname soon changed to Tanni.

Shami Chakrabarti

Born: 1969, London

Lawyer, human rights activist

Shami Chakrabarti studied law at the London School of Economics. She became a lawyer in the Home Office (a government department) in 1996. While there, Chakrabarti worked on the Human Rights Act. She began work at Liberty, the human rights' organization, in 2001. By 2003, she was its director (leader). She left Liberty in 2016 and is now a member of the Labour Party in the House of Lords.

Dame Kelly Holmes

Born: 1970, Pembury, Kent

Athlete

Kelly Holmes joined the British Army in 1987 as a lorry driver. She later became an Army Physical Training Instructor. In 1997, Holmes decided to focus on athletics full time. In 2004, Holmes achieved her childhood dream and won two Olympic gold medals, for the 800 metres and 1500 metres. She  was chosen by British sports fans as the BBC Sports Personality of the Year that year. Holmes retired from athletics in 2005. In 2008 she started the Dame Kelly Holmes Legacy Trust, which supports young athletes.

Dame Ellen MacArthur

Born: 1976, Whatstandwell, Derbyshire

Long-distance sailor, author

Ellen MacArthur began sailing at a young age. In 1995, she sailed around Britain on her own, which won her the Young Sailor of the Year Award. In 2001, she raced single-handedly non-stop around the world in the Vendée Globe race. She finished second but was the youngest person to ever finish the race. MacArthur set a world record time for her single-handed round-the-world voyage in 2005. She was made a Dame later that year. MacArthur retired from sailing in 2009.

landmine explosive device that explodes when someone steps on it

landscape painting painting that focuses on views of the countryside

Member of Parliament (MP) person chosen by the people in a particular area to represent their interests in Parliament

missionary Christian sent to a foreign country in order to teach people there about Christianity

naturalist person who studies the natural world, such as plants and insects

palaeontologist person who studies fossils

patent official right given to an inventor to make or sell his or her invention without it being copied by others

penicillin type of drug called an antibiotic, which is used in the treatment of infections and disease-causing bacteria

physicist person who studies matter and energy

physics study of matter and energy

playwright person who writes plays

Poet Laureate poet asked to write poems for special occasions such as a royal wedding

politician person who is involved in the governing of a country, as a Member of Parliament

Pope head of the Roman Catholic Church

primatologist person who studies primates, such as chimpanzees and monkeys

profession job that requires special training

prosthetic artificial limb

radiation rays of energy given off by certain elements

radio pulsars spinning neutron stars that give out bursts of radiation

rank someone's position within a rank or organization

reform changes or improvements to a system or law

Romantic movement in poetry, it meant expressing feelings through writing

sculptor person who carves or moulds figures or shapes from stone, metal, wood or other materials

socialist person who believes in an economic system in which the goods made by factories, businesses and farms are controlled by the government

structure how something is made or built

suffragette woman who took part in the fight for women's right to vote

surveyor person who examines land or buildings in order to check their condition

vaccine medicine that prevents disease

Vikings people from Norway and Denmark who attacked Britain from the late AD 700s

X-ray crystallographer person who works out the structure of a substance by passing a beam of X-rays through it and analysing the patterns

zoology the study of animals

Glossary

abolition formal ending of something, usually by law

admiral senior officer in the Royal Navy

anonymous not identified by name; of unknown name

apothecary person who prepares medicines

architect person who designs and draws plans for buildings, bridges and other construction projects

astronomy study of stars, planets and space

baroness woman who is a member of the lowest rank of nobility

brand name that identifies a product or manufacturer, such as Adidas

campaigner person who works in an organized way in order to reach a goal, such as improving the rights of a particular group of people

cartographer person who draws or creates maps

chemist person who studies the structure of substances and the way they react with other substances

Children's Laureate writer or illustrator of children's books who is honoured for their contribution to children's publishing

co-founded when more than one person is involved in setting up an organization or charity

cosmologist person who studies the beginning of the universe

coxed in rowing, a cox gives instructions to the rowers as they row

debt money that a person owes

DNA material in cells that gives people their individual characteristics; DNA stands for deoxyribonucleic acid

electromagnetism magnetism produced by an electric current

engineer person who uses science and maths to plan, build and maintain buildings, bridges and other construction projects

entrepreneur person who takes financial risks to start up new business opportunities

fossil remains or traces of plants and animals that are preserved as rock

governess person who teaches children in a family household

ground engineer person who determines whether a plane is safe to fly

human rights activist person who campaigns for everyone to have basic rights, such as food, water and shelter

Impressionism style of painting that shows the mood or effects of light on a landscape rather than how it looks in detail

insulin hormone created by a part of the body called the pancreas. Insulin controls the amount of glucose (a form of sugar) in the blood stream. People with diabetes are unable to produce enough insulin.

knighted when a person is made a "Sir" by the king or queen

David Walliams

Born: 1971, London

Author, actor, comedian

At the age of 19, David Williams (he later changed his surname to Walliams) met Matt Lucas at the National Youth Theatre. In 2003, the sketch show *Little Britain* became a hit for Walliams and Lucas. In 2006, Walliams swam the English Channel for Sport Relief. He raised over £1 million. Walliams began writing children's books in 2008, including *Billionaire Boy* (2010) and *Gangsta Granny* (2011). By the end of 2014, he had sold around 4 million copies. Walliams joined the TV talent show *Britain's Got Talent* as a judge in 2012.

FAST FACT

Quentin Blake, the artist who illustrated Roald Dahl's books, worked on some of Walliams' novels.

Sir Andy Murray

Born: 1987, Glasgow

Tennis player

Andy Murray played tennis from a young age. He became a professional tennis player in 2005, but it wasn't until 2012 that he won his first Grand Slam event: the US Open. In 2013, Murray became the first British man to win Wimbledon since Fred Perry in 1936. Murray was a member of the British team that won the Davis Cup in 2015. Another Wimbledon win in 2016 led to him becoming the number one ranked player in the world. Murray also has two Olympic gold medals, from 2012 and 2016. These achievements led to him being knighted by the queen in 2017.

Sir Lenny Henry

Born: 1958, Dudley, West Midlands

Comedian, actor, writer

Lenny Henry appeared on a TV talent show called *New Faces* when he was just 16 years old. Since then, he has appeared in many television programmes and films, performed on stage and continued to do stand-up comedy shows around the world. Henry is also well known for his charity work, having co-founded Comic Relief in 1985. Comic Relief uses comedy to raise money to help those in need in Africa and the UK. The first Red Nose Day took place in 1988 and the first Sport Relief in 2002.

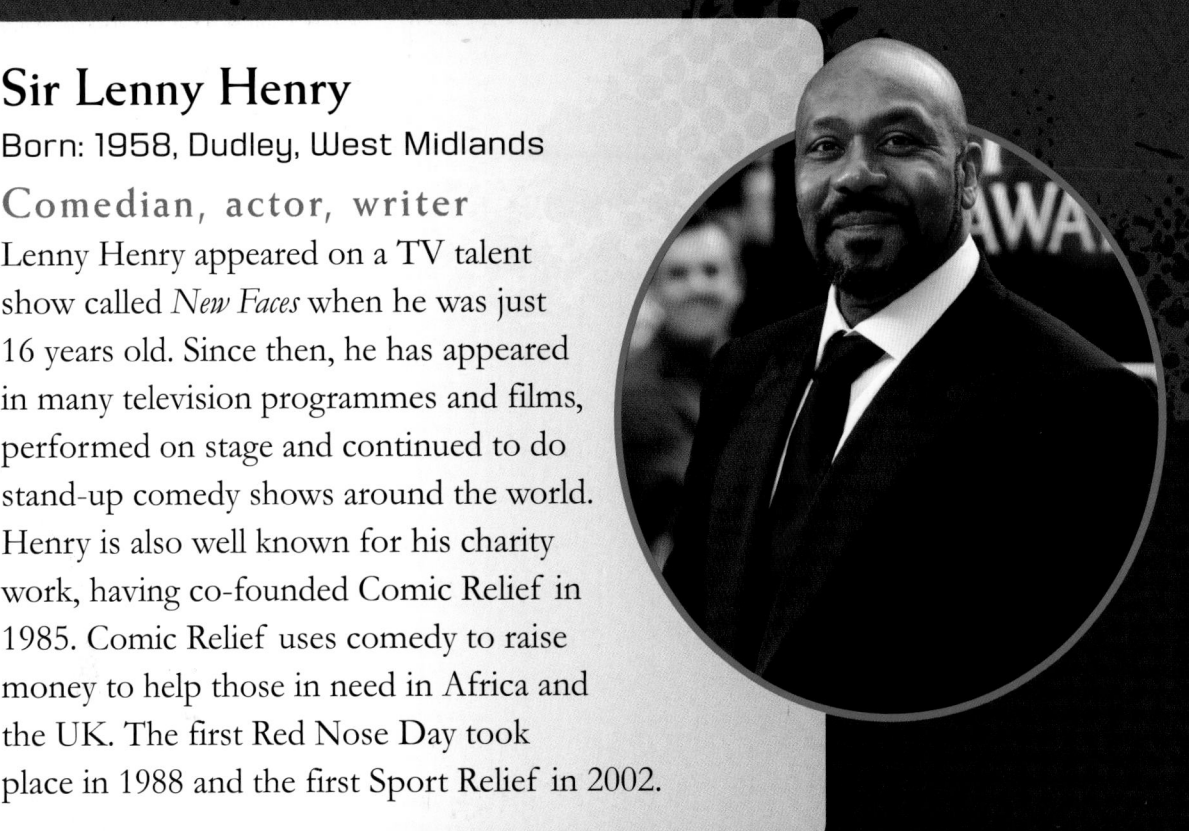

Sir Steve Redgrave

Born: 1962, Marlow, Buckinghamshire

Rower

Steve Redgrave started rowing at the age of 16. Soon, he was representing Great Britain at the World Junior Championships. At the 1984 Olympics in Los Angeles, USA, Redgrave won his first gold medal in the **coxed** fours race. He changed to the coxless pairs event for the next Olympics, but the result was the same: gold. More golds followed after a change of partner (to Matthew Pinsent). He retired in 1996, but was tempted back to the coxless fours. In 2000, Redgrave won gold for the fifth Olympics in a row. He was knighted in 2001 and went on to become a rowing commentator for TV.

Sir Richard Branson

Born: 1950, London

Businessman, entrepreneur

In 1970, Richard Branson set up his new company, Virgin, selling records through the post. The next step was to open a record shop called Virgin Records in London. Branson then decided to record music too. Mike Oldfield's *Tubular Bells* was the first album recorded. Branson expanded the Virgin **brand** by creating Virgin flights, holidays, hotels and train journeys. He is even working on trips into space! Branson set up Virgin Unite in 2004. Virgin Unite helps others set up their own businesses and tackles environmental and social problems.

Sir Tim Berners-Lee

Born: 1955, London

Engineer, computer scientist

Tim Berners-Lee studied Physics at Oxford University. It was while working at CERN (European Particle Physics Laboratory) in 1989 that Berners-Lee came up with the idea of sharing information via computer. At CERN, to find out something, a scientist had to log on to the computer that contained that information. They weren't able to access it from a different computer. Berners-Lee created a program that would convert the information to allow access from any computer. He had invented the World Wide Web. He was able to do this because other people had invented things like hypertext, a way of connecting one document to another.

Bobby Moore

Born: 1941, Barking, Essex
Died: 1993, London

Footballer

Bobby Moore enjoyed playing cricket as a boy, but eventually decided he wanted to be a footballer. He first played for West Ham United as a defender in 1958. He went on to play in over 500 matches for the team. In 1966, Moore captained England in the World Cup. England won the competition and Moore was seen as a national hero. He captained England 90 times. Moore left West Ham in 1974 to play for Fulham. After his playing career ended, he went into football management and radio football commentary.

Stephen Hawking

Born: 1942, Oxford

Physicist, **cosmologist**, author

Stephen Hawking studied at Oxford University. At the age of 21, Hawking discovered he had motor neurone disease. Doctors told him he had just two years to live. Hearing this caused him to focus on his studies. By 1966, Hawking was studying the beginnings of the universe and black holes. His best-known discovery is that black holes give off **radiation**. This is now known as Hawking radiation. Despite his declining health, Hawking has spent much of his career trying to find a theory that explains our universe. He has written many science books, including *A Brief History of Time* (1988). Hawking has also written children's books with his daughter.

James Watson, Francis Crick and Maurice Wilkins

Francis born: 1916, Weston Favell, Northamptonshire
Died: 2004, San Diego, USA

Maurice born: 1916, Pongaroa, New Zealand
Died: 2004, London

James born: 1928, Chicago, USA

Scientists

In the early 1950s, scientists Maurice Wilkins and Rosalind Franklin were investigating X-ray photographs of **DNA** samples. Scientists James Watson and Francis Crick were also studying DNA. Watson had degrees in **zoology** and had become interested in DNA after hearing Wilkins give a talk about the **structure** of DNA. Crick was a **physicist**. In 1953, they were able to work out that the structure of DNA is a double helix, or ladder. They had worked from an X-ray photograph produced by Franklin. In 1962, Watson, Crick and Wilkins were awarded the Nobel Prize.

Sir David Attenborough

Born: 1926, London

Naturalist, TV presenter

David Attenborough studied Natural Sciences at Cambridge University. He worked at the BBC from 1965, introducing the popular series *Zoo Quest*. In 1972, he left the BBC to work for himself. He then began to present nature programmes. About 500 million people around the world watched *Life on Earth*, Attenborough's 1979 TV series. Later TV series demonstrated Attenborough's interest in environmental issues.

FAST FACT

Early on in his career, a boss at the BBC decided Attenborough shouldn't be on screen because his teeth were too big!

Sir Douglas Bader

Born: 1910, London
Died: 1982, London

RAF pilot

Douglas Bader became an officer in
the Royal Air Force (RAF) in 1930.
A year later, he lost both his legs in a
plane crash. He was walking again, on
prosthetic legs, within six months.
Despite the fact that Bader showed
he could still fly, he was forced to

leave the RAF. When World War II began, Bader re-joined the RAF. He was
shot down and imprisoned by the Germans. Despite his disability, Bader
continually tried to escape. He returned to England when the war ended.
After the war, Bader was an inspiration to others with disabilities. He was
knighted in 1976.

Roald Dahl

Born: 1916, Llandaff, Wales
Died: 1990, Oxford

Author, poet, screenwriter, fighter pilot, spy

Roald Dahl joined the Royal Air Force as a pilot at the start of
World War II. He later acted as a spy for the British government.
Dahl began his writing career while living in the United States. He is
best known for his children's stories, such as *Charlie and the Chocolate
Factory* (1964) and *The BFG* (1982). He wrote for films too, such as
Chitty Chitty Bang Bang (1968). His
stories for adults, which were made
into a television series in the 1980s,
were often scary.

FAST FACT

Roald Dahl was named after a
Norwegian explorer called Roald
Amundsen. Amundsen was the first
man to reach the South Pole.

Aneurin Bevan

Born: 1897, Tredegar, South Wales
Died: 1960, Chesham, Buckinghamshire

Politician

Aneurin Bevan worked in coal mines from the age of 13. Bevan was one of the leaders of the South Wales miners during the 1926 General Strike. Three years later, Bevan was chosen as the Labour member of parliament (MP) for Ebbw Vale. In 1945, Labour won the general election and Bevan was made minister of health. He was responsible for setting up the National Health Service from 1948. In 1955, Bevan was beaten in his attempt to become Labour Party leader. Four years later, he was made deputy leader, but he died shortly afterwards.

Laurence Olivier

Born: 1907, Dorking, Surrey
Died: 1989, Steyning, West Sussex

Actor

Laurence Olivier began his career as a theatre actor and was particularly well known for performing Shakespeare's plays. He married actress Vivien Leigh in 1940, and they often performed together on stage. In 1962, Olivier helped to set up the Royal National Theatre in London and was its director until 1973. His main love was theatre but he also appeared in many films, such as *Wuthering Heights* (1939) and *Rebecca* (1940). He won a Best Actor Oscar for the film version of *Hamlet* in 1949. Olivier was **knighted** in 1947.

Charles Dickens

Born: 1812, Portsmouth
Died: 1870, Kent

Author

Author Charles Dickens' parents had been imprisoned for **debt** when he was 12 years old. Dickens then had to work in a factory for three years. He used this experience in many of his later writings about working conditions for the poor. Dickens wrote 15 novels, including *Oliver Twist* (1838) and *Great Expectations* (1861). Many of his novels were in the form of serials, where a number of chapters were released each week.

David Livingstone

Born: 1813, Blantyre, South Lanarkshire
Died: 1873, Chitambo (now Zambia)

Explorer, missionary, anti-slavery campaigner

David Livingstone trained as a doctor and a missionary. He went to Africa in 1841, travelling from one side of the continent to the other. He discovered many places that no European had seen before, such as the Zambezi River. Livingstone hated the slave trade after seeing the cruel way in which African slaves were treated. From 1864, he campaigned against it. He made a final trip to Africa in 1866. He died there while attempting to find the source of the River Nile.

Robert Thomson and John Boyd Dunlop

Robert born: 1822, Stonehaven, Kincardineshire
Died: 1873, Edinburgh

John born: 1840, Dreghorn, Ayrshire
Died: 1921, Dublin, Ireland

Engineer, vet, inventor

Robert Thomson got a patent for the air-filled tyre, known as the pneumatic tyre, in France (1846) and in the United States (1847). He had invented the "aerial wheel" to make carriage rides quieter and more comfortable. However, few people wanted to buy tyres at this time, as cars hadn't been invented and bicycles weren't very common.

Forty years later, John Boyd Dunlop, a vet living in Belfast, Northern Ireland, re-invented the pneumatic tyre. He tested the tyre on his son's tricycle – and it worked! The following year, Dunlop took out a patent on it. Soon his tyres were in use everywhere, including on the new motor vehicles.

Alexander Graham Bell

Born: 1847, Edinburgh
Died: 1922, Cape Breton Island, Nova Scotia, Canada

Inventor, scientist

Alexander Graham Bell, whose mother was deaf, began studying how speech works from the age of 16. In 1870, Bell's family moved to Canada. He taught deaf children and also teachers of the deaf. Bell was interested in sending speech through wires. He worked with an engineer called Thomas Watson and together they created the first telephone in 1876. Bell got a patent for the device and carried out a public demonstration three months later. The Bell Telephone Company was set up in 1877.

FAST FACT

By the time Bell died, about 13 million telephones were in use around the world.

Captain Robert F. Scott

Born: 1868, Devonport, Devon
Died: 1912, Antarctica

Explorer

Robert F. Scott was an officer in the Royal
Navy during the 1880s and 1890s. The Royal
Geographical Society then made him leader of
the National Antarctic Expedition of 1901–1904.
This expedition got further south than anyone had ever
managed before. Scott was seen as a hero. He decided he wanted to be
the first man to reach the South Pole. In 1910, Scott and his team set
off on the ship *Terra Nova*. They had to deal with terrible conditions in
the cold and ice. Devastatingly, once they reached the Pole, they found
that a Norwegian team had got there first. All five of Scott's team died
on the return journey.

Sir Winston Churchill

Born: 1874, Blenheim, Oxfordshire
Died: 1965, London

Politician, Prime Minister, author

Winston Churchill was a soldier and a journalist in his early adult
life. He became a Member of Parliament (MP) in 1900 for the
Conservative Party. Churchill made some bad decisions early on in
his political career, and was forced to resign after Britain lost many
soldiers at Gallipoli during World War I (1914–1918). In 1940, during
World War II (1939–1945), Churchill was chosen to be Prime Minister.
He gave many inspiring speeches and worked hard to ensure that
Britain won the war. Labour won the election of 1946, but in 1951 the
Conservatives won and Churchill was Prime Minister once more. By
this time, though, he was old and ill, and he resigned in 1955.

Sir Alexander Fleming

Born: 1881, Lochfield, Ayrshire
Died: 1955, London

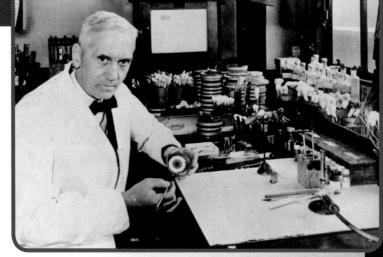

Scientist

Alexander Fleming qualified as a doctor at St Mary's Medical School, London University. He worked as a researcher there and returned to St Mary's after serving in the Royal Army Medical Corps during World War I. In 1928, while studying flu, he found that a dish used to grow a germ called *staphylococci* had developed mould. There was a ring around it that was bacteria-free. After more experimenting, Fleming realized he had found something important. He called it **penicillin**. Scientists Howard Florey and Ernst Chain developed the substance and produced it as a drug to kill infections. Fleming, Florey and Chain shared the 1945 Nobel Prize in Medicine.

John Logie Baird

Born: 1888, Helensburgh, Argyll and Bute
Died: 1946, Bexhill-on-Sea, Sussex

Engineer, inventor

John Logie Baird worked as an engineer and a salesman, before moving to England in 1922. There, he built the first television with bits and bobs, including an old hatbox! In January 1926, Baird first demonstrated moving pictures on a screen. In 1927, he set up the Baird Television Development Company. A television picture was broadcast from Britain to the United States in 1928. Baird also produced the first colour TV signal. His way of sending TV pictures was soon outdated, though. Electronic versions were developed by the Marconi-EMI company.

Isambard Kingdom Brunel

Born: 1806, Portsmouth
Died: 1859, London

Engineer

Early in his career, Isambard Kingdom Brunel worked with his father on planning the Thames Tunnel in London. In 1831, Brunel's design was chosen for the Clifton Suspension Bridge in Bristol. He was just 24 years old at the time.

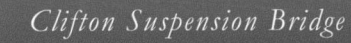

Clifton Suspension Bridge

Brunel is best known for designing the Great Western Railway from London and Bristol. He also designed the Great Western steamship, which travelled between Britain and the United States.

Charles Darwin

Born: 1809, Shrewsbury, Shropshire
Died: 1882, Downe, Kent

Naturalist, author

Charles Darwin first studied to be a doctor. He then changed his mind and tried the church. But Darwin's life changed when he joined the ship HMS *Beagle* as a naturalist. He later wrote about his travels around the world. Darwin is best known for his theory of evolution. He said that creatures change their form over time to adapt to their surroundings – only the strongest and best suited to their environment survive. His book *On the Origin of Species* was published in 1859.

Sir Robert Peel

Born: 1788, Bury, Lancashire
Died: 1850, London

Politician

Sir Robert Peel became a Member of Parliament (MP) in 1809. In 1829, as part of a **reform** of criminal law, he created the Metropolitan Police Force in London. He was Prime Minister for the Tory Party in 1834–1835. In 1839, Prime Minister Lord Melbourne (of the Whig Party) was forced to resign over a political issue. Peel was to be the new Prime Minister. He asked Queen Victoria to change some of her ladies-in-waiting because they were all married to Whigs. She refused. Peel knew he didn't have her support, so Lord Melbourne had to continue as Prime Minister. Peel became Prime Minister for the second time in 1841.

FAST FACT

"Bobbies" is a nickname sometimes used for police officers. It comes from Sir Robert's name.

Michael Faraday

Born: 1791, Newington, Surrey   Died: 1867, Molesey, Surrey

Scientist

After hearing talks by famous scientist Humphry Davy in 1812, Michael Faraday wrote to him asking to be his assistant. Davy said no, but the next year, he gave Faraday a job at the Royal Institution in London. Faraday is best known for his experiments in electricity and magnetism. He was the first person to make an electric current from a magnetic field. In 1831, he discovered **electromagnetic** induction; this allowed electricity to be used as a new source of power.

J.M.W. Turner

Born: 1775, London
Died: 1851, London

Artist

Joseph Mallord William Turner studied art at the Royal Academy schools. By 1804, Turner had his own studio and gallery where he could work and show his paintings. Turner

Keelmen Heaving in Coals by Moonlight, *1835*

was well known for **landscape painting**, particularly of views of the sea. At first, his paintings were very detailed, but he later focused more on light and colour. Some people think that his later style inspired **Impressionist** artists such as Claude Monet.

George and Robert Stephenson

George born: 1781, Wylam
Died: 1848, Chesterfield

Robert born: 1803, Willington Quay
Died: 1859, London

Engineers

In 1825, George Stephenson built the first passenger steam railway in the world – the Stockton to Darlington railway. Stephenson built the track as well. He used a "standard gauge", which was a set width for all train tracks. It is still used today. In 1829, George's son, Robert, helped his father build the *Rocket*, a train used for the Liverpool to Manchester railway line. Robert built railways all over the world and bridges too, including the Britannia Bridge in Wales.

William Wilberforce

Born: 1759, Hull, Yorkshire
Died: 1833, London

Anti-slavery campaigner

William Wilberforce was a **Member of Parliament (MP)** from 1780. In 1787, he helped to set up the Anti-Slavery Society. The slave trade involved the capturing, buying and selling of people as slaves. At this time, African slaves worked on sugar plantations in the West Indies. These lands were controlled by Britain. Wilberforce spent a number of years trying to push through an anti-slavery law in Parliament. British trade in slaves was finally ended in 1807. From 1821 to his retirement in 1825, Wilberforce worked to give all slaves their freedom. Three days before he died, the Slavery **Abolition** Act was finally passed. This made any slave trading across the British Empire illegal.

William Wordsworth

Born: 1770, Cockermouth, Cumbria
Died: 1850, Ambleside, Cumbria

Poet

William Wordsworth loved nature and wrote poems as a schoolboy. His early poems were published in 1793. He produced *Lyrical Ballads* with poet Samuel Taylor Coleridge in 1798. This was thought to be the start of the **Romantic movement** in English poetry. In 1799, Wordsworth and his wife and sister moved to Grasmere. Here, he wrote his best-known poem, "I Wandered Lonely as a Cloud". In 1843, Wordsworth was made **Poet Laureate**.

John McAdam and Edgar Hooley

John born: 1756, Ayr, Ayrshire   Died: 1836, Moffat, Dumfriesshire
Edgar born: 1860, Swansea   Died: 1942, Oxford

Engineer; surveyor

John McAdam made his fortune in America. On his return to Britain, he came up with a new way to build roads. He suggested building them higher than the land around them, so rain could drain away, and covering the surface in small stones. McAdam's method – macadamisation – was used throughout Britain, Europe and America. However, McAdam hadn't been able to get the stones to stick. A surveyor called Edgar Hooley came up with a solution. A barrel of tar had spilled on to a road and waste material from coal mining (called slag) had been put on top to tidy it up. Hooley noticed how smooth the road was. After experimenting with mixing tar and slag, Hooley got a **patent** for Tarmac in 1902. The business he set up to sell it failed. So he decided to sell the company. But today, tarmac is used to cover all road surfaces.

Vice-Admiral Horatio Nelson

Born: 1758, Burnham Thorpe, Norfolk
Died: 1805, HMS *Victory*, Cape Trafalgar, Spain

Navy **Admiral**

Horatio Nelson joined the Royal Navy in 1770. He was a captain by the age of 20. He gradually worked his way up the **ranks**, despite the fact that he didn't always follow orders. Britain was at war with France from 1793. Nelson and his men won some very important sea battles, including the Nile (1798) and Copenhagen (1801). Nelson was made Vice-Admiral in 1801. Victory at the Battle of Trafalgar in 1805 saved Britain from a French invasion. But it was during this battle that Nelson was shot and killed.

FAST FACT

During the Battle of Calvi in 1794, Nelson lost the sight in his right eye. He lost his right arm in battle in 1797.

Captain James Cook

Born: 1728, Middlesbrough
Died: 1779, Kealakekua Bay, Hawaii

Explorer, cartographer

In 1755, James Cook joined the Royal Navy. In 1769, the British government put Cook in charge of the ship HMS *Endeavour*. Cook and his men became the first Europeans to see New Zealand and Australia. Cook claimed the east coast of Australia for Britain and called it New South Wales. Another journey for Cook involved searching for the Northwest Passage, which was thought to link the Pacific and Atlantic Oceans. Unable to find it, Cook went to explore Hawaii. The sailors were welcomed by the local people. However, on a return journey, a riot broke out and Cook was killed by the locals.

Edward Jenner

Born: 1749, Berkeley, Gloucestershire
Died: 1823, Berkeley, Gloucestershire

Doctor, scientist

In 1770, Edward Jenner went to London to train as a doctor. Two years later, he returned home as the local doctor. Jenner was interested in the fact that dairymaids who had had cowpox didn't seem to catch the deadly disease smallpox. Cowpox was a mild disease caught by many who worked with cows. Jenner experimented by placing a tiny amount of cowpox into a cut on a young boy's arm. The boy got cowpox, but when Jenner did the same with smallpox, the boy didn't get ill. Having had cowpox, he was protected. Jenner had created a smallpox **vaccine**. Jenner became famous around the world for his discovery, but he remained a country doctor.

Alfred the Great

Born: AD 849, Wantage
Died: AD 899, Winchester

Anglo-Saxon king

In AD 871, Alfred the Great helped his brother, the king of Wessex, to defeat the **Vikings** at the Battle of Ashdown. After becoming king in AD 872, Alfred was pushed back to the Somerset marshes by the Vikings. But he again defeated the Vikings at the Battle of Edington in AD 878. A peace agreement was made called the Danelaw. The Danelaw split England into land for the Vikings and land for the English. To prepare for further attacks, Alfred organized his army, created a navy and strengthened towns. Alfred also improved education and brought together important laws for his kingdom.

Athelstan

Born: AD 895, unknown
Died: AD 939, Gloucester

First king of England

Athelstan was crowned king of England in AD 925. He was a great soldier, and it was said that he never lost a battle. The northern city of York had been under the control of the Vikings since AD 866. Athelstan regained York for England in AD 927–928. In AD 934, Athelstan was described as "king of the English", the first to be given that title. Athelstan's defeat of the Scots at the Battle of Brunanburh in AD 937 helped to bring the different tribes of England together.

Edward the Confessor

Born: 1003, Islip, Oxfordshire
Died: 1066, London

Anglo-Saxon king

Edward the Confessor became king in 1042. He had lived in Normandy, France, for much of his life while Danish kings ruled England. His reign was peaceful until he introduced Normans into important roles at court. Other nobles weren't happy, especially Godwine, Earl of Wessex, who rebelled. The king was forced to send his Norman friends away. After Godwine died, his son Harold became one of Edward's favourites. It is thought that Edward said Harold should be the next king. However, he may also have promised William of Normandy the throne. This confusion led to William and his Norman army invading England in 1066.

Robert the Bruce

Born: 1274, Ayrshire
Died: 1329, Cardross, Dumbartonshire

King of the Scots

Robert the Bruce came from a family that had claims to the Scottish throne. King Edward I of England had made himself king of Scotland in 1296. But the Scots, led by William Wallace, rebelled and won a major battle at Stirling Bridge in 1297. Wallace was captured and killed. This allowed Robert to declare himself king in 1306. In 1314, Robert defeated the English king Edward II at the Battle of Bannockburn. However, Edward II didn't give up his claim to the Scottish throne. In 1320 the Scots asked the **Pope** to judge. In 1324, the Pope agreed that Robert was the rightful king of Scotland.

William Shakespeare

Born: 1564, Stratford-upon-Avon,
    Warwickshire
Died: 1616, Stratford-upon-Avon,
    Warwickshire

Poet, playwright, actor

After getting married and having three children, William Shakespeare left his family in Stratford and moved to London. He worked as an actor and **playwright** for the Lord Chamberlain's Men. Shakespeare wrote many plays, but their dates are not known exactly. It is thought that they were being performed on the London stage by 1592. Shakespeare's works have been translated into 80 languages and over 4 billion copies of his plays and poetry have been sold. More than 400 films have been made of his plays, with *Hamlet* and *Romeo and Juliet* being the most popular.

Sir Christopher Wren

Born: 1632, East Knoyle, Wiltshire
Died: 1723, London

Scientist, mathematician, **architect**

Christopher Wren's early career was in **astronomy**. He was Professor of Astronomy at Gresham College in London from 1657. There, in 1660, Wren **co-founded** the Royal Society, the oldest scientific society in the world. From 1662, Wren turned his attentions to architecture. After the Great Fire of London in 1666, Wren put forward a design for a new St Paul's Cathedral to replace the old one. After a long time, in 1711, the building was finally finished.

Sir Isaac Newton

Born: 1643, Woolsthorpe, Lincolnshire
Died: 1727, London

Scientist, mathematician, astronomer

Sir Isaac Newton studied at Cambridge University and became a Professor of Mathematics there. He is best known for the ideas in his book *Philosophiae Naturalis Principia Mathematica*, published in 1687. The book included Newton's ideas about calculus (a form of maths), the laws of motion and gravity. His laws of motion formed the basis of the science of **physics**. Newton's ideas about gravity helped to explain the movements of planets. The story goes that he was inspired to think about gravity after watching an apple fall from a tree. Newton experimented all his life and invented new devices, such as the reflecting telescope. He was a member of the Royal Society, a group of top scientists, and president of it from 1703.

Lancelot "Capability" Brown

Born: 1716, Kirkharle,
    Northumberland
Died: 1783, London

Garden designer

Lancelot Brown worked for Lord Cobham at Stowe House and was head gardener by the age of 26. Many of Lord Cobham's friends asked Brown to design their gardens. He created the gardens

Stowe landscape garden

at Burghley House and Blenheim Palace. Brown was then made Master Gardener at Hampton Court Palace in 1764. Brown's gardens were designed to be natural-looking and "unplanned". It is believed that he worked on 170 gardens.

Great British

Men

raintree

a Capstone company — publishers for children

Raintree is an imprint of Capstone Global Library Limited, a company incorporated in England and Wales having its registered office at 7 Pilgrim Street, London, EC4V 6LB – Registered company number: 6695582

www.raintree.co.uk
myorders@raintree.co.uk

Text © Capstone Global Library Limited 2018
The moral rights of the proprietor have been asserted.

Edited by Helen Cox Cannons, Designed by Cynthia Della-Rovere, Picture research by Svetlana Zhurkin, Production by Kathy McColley
Originated by Capstone Global Library Limited
Printed and bound in India

ISBN 978 1 4747 5494 1
22 21 20 19 18
10 9 8 7 6 5 4 3 2 1

British Library Cataloguing in Publication Data
A full catalogue record for this book is available from the British Library.

Acknowledgements
On the cover of Great British Men (left to right): William Shakespeare, Sir Winston Churchill, Sir David Attenborough; on the cover of Great British Women (left to right): Florence Nightingale, Queen Elizabeth II, Boudicca

Image credits

Great British Men:
Alamy: Universal Art Archive, cover (left), 1 (left); AP Photo: Press Association/David Parry, cover (right), 1 (right); iStockphoto: duncan1890, 8; Library of Congress, 16; Newscom: Mirrorpix, 17, NI Syndication, 18, Zuma Press/Andrew Couldridge, 23; Shutterstock: Chrispo, 3, Claudio Divizia, 12, Everett Art, 10 (top), Everett Historical, 5, 13, Featureflash Photo Agency, 22, Georgios Kollidas, 7, 9, 11, Kathy Hutchins, 21, Koca Vehbi, 20, Oleg Golovnev, 15, Patrick Wang, 6, Rachelle Burnside, 4, vitstudio, 19, Yangchao, 10 (bottom); SuperStock: cover (middle), 1 (middle)

Great British Women:
Alamy: Art Collection 2, 9, Lebrecht Music and Arts Photo Library, cover (right), 1 (right); Dreamstime: Georgios Kollidas, 5; Getty Images: Corbis/Hulton-Deutsch Collection, 8, Library of Congress, cover (left), 1 (left), 4, 10; Newscom: Allstar/Sportsphoto, 23, Mirrorpix, 15, NI Syndication, 13, Photoshot/Retna/Jules Annan, 21, Pictures From History, 12, Sipa Press/Pascal Saez, 19, Zuma Press/Gareth Copley, 22; Shutterstock: AC Manley, 14, Everett Art, 3, 7, Tinseltown, 17, Twocoms, 18; SuperStock: Marka, cover (middle), 1 (middle); Wikimedia: Government Art Collection, 6, Margaret Thatcher Foundation, 16

Design Elements by Shutterstock

Every effort has been made to contact copyright holders of material reproduced in this book. Any omissions will be rectified in subsequent printings if notice is given to the publisher.

All the internet addresses (URLs) given in this book were valid at the time of going to press. However, due to the dynamic nature of the internet, some addresses may have changed, or sites may have changed or ceased to exist since publication. While the author and publisher regret any inconvenience this may cause readers, no responsibility for any such changes can be accepted by either the author or the publisher.

ENTRIES ARE COLOUR CODED IN THE FOLLOWING CATEGORIES:

- ACTORS/MUSICIANS/SINGERS
- ADVENTURERS/EXPLORERS
- ARCHITECTS/ENGINEERS
- ARTISTS/SCULPTORS
- AUTHORS/POETS/WRITERS
- BUSINESS/COMPUTING
- DESIGNERS
- MEDICAL/SOCIAL CAMPAIGNERS
- MILITARY
- POLITICS
- ROYALTY
- SCIENTISTS
- SPORTSPEOPLE